Catalogue Of A Collection Of Woodcuts Of The German School: Executed In The Fifteenth And Sixteenth Centuries

J. M.

In the interest of creating a more extensive selection of rare historical book reprints, we have chosen to reproduce this title even though it may possibly have occasional imperfections such as missing and blurred pages, missing text, poor pictures, markings, dark backgrounds and other reproduction issues beyond our control. Because this work is culturally important, we have made it available as a part of our commitment to protecting, preserving and promoting the world's literature. Thank you for your understanding.

Burlington Fine Arts Club.

CATALOGUE

OF A

COLLECTION OF WOODCUTS

OF THE GERMAN SCHOOL,

EXECUTED IN THE XVTH AND XVITH CENTURIES.

LONDON:

PRINTED FOR THE BURLINGTON FINE ARTS CLUB.

1882.

EXHIBITION

OF A

COLLECTION OF WOODCUTS.

INTRODUCTION.

THE art of engraving designs on wooden blocks, so as to obtain from them impressions or reproductions of those designs upon paper, by means of printers' ink, though unknown to the Romans, who yet knew how to stamp cyphers and marks upon their bricks, and though partially developed among the Chinese and Japanese as early as the Xth century, does not appear to have been practised in Europe before the close of the XIIth century. It began in Germany, and is supposed to have owed its introduction to the use of playing-cards, brought into Europe from the East, and said to have been invented by the Arabs. These seem to have been first known in Italy, as is indicated by their name, derived from the Italian *carte*, about 1350. From that country their popularity spread very quickly in all

INTRODUCTION.

directions, and especially towards Germany, where there soon grew up a large trade in them, but not much before the close of the XIVth century.

That the first European practice of this art was in Germany, is hardly to be doubted. All the earliest examples hitherto discovered point to a German origin; and nowhere was the art more rapidly developed, or brought to a higher pitch of excellence, than in the land of its adoption.

The object, therefore, of giving, within a reasonable compass, an illustration of the history of wood-engraving from the middle of the XVth to the end of the XVIth century could not be, perhaps, better attained than by assembling a select collection of the works, executed in wood, of some representative artists of the German schools which flourished during that period. This it has been attempted to accomplish in the present Exhibition.

It is not considered likely that many, if any, of these painters and designers executed their cuts with their own hands upon the blocks; this, rather the work of artisans than of artists, was probably in most cases relegated to persons who were specially fitted for the mechanical performance, and who worked under the direction and supervision of the originators of the designs. In some cases these executants signed the blocks as well with their own as with the master's name; as, for example, Jost de Negker (Cat. 91), who seems to have cut many of Burgmair's blocks; in others, as on the little cut, "Die Herzogin" (Cat. 127), with their own name only.

The chronological, the only rational, order of arrangement has been followed, in placing the artists, as far as the sequence of their dates could be ascertained. To place the works of each in chronological sequence would be a task of almost insuperable difficulty, owing to the fact of those works having been executed by different hands, which fact alone would be quite enough to mask the development of style, to illustrate which is the only and the grand aim of the chronological system. This, therefore, had to be foregone; and the prints are placed nearly according to the arbitrary arrangement adopted by Bartsch, Passavant, and other writers.

J. M.

The indications (B.) and (Pass.) in the Catalogue refer to the lists of Bartsch and Passavant.

The prints and books of which this Collection consists have been contributed by three members of the Club,

Mr. R. Fisher,
Mr. H. H. Gibbs,
Mr. W. Mitchell.

INDEX.

	PAGE
Altdorfer, Albrecht	12
Amman, Jost	20
Anonymous	1,2
Beham, Hans Sebald	18
Burgmair, Hans	8
Cranach, Lucas	2
Deutsch, Nicolas Manuel	10
Dürer, Albrecht	4-8
Geron, Mathias	20
Graf, Urse	11
Grün, Hans Baldung	10
Holbein, Ambrosius	13
Holbein, Hans	15-18
Hopfer, Daniel	14
Loy, Erasmus	20
Ostendorfer, Michael	13
Pleydenwurff, Wilhelm	2
Reuwich, Erhard	1
Schäufelein, Hans Leonhard	11
Springinklee, Hans	14
Wechtlin, or Wächtle, Johann	12
Wohlgemuth, Michael	2

CATALOGUE.

ANONYMOUS.

1.—Christ on the Cross (coloured).

Described by Passavant (T. I. p. 22) among the earliest specimens of wood-cuts executed for monasteries, in the first half of the XVth century. This was engraved, probably, for the Monastery of Tegernsee, in Bavaria, whose arms appear upon it.

It is curious and interesting to note, in the prints of this epoch, with their heavy outlines and antiquity of appearance, at the same time the rounded folds of the draperies, as contrasted with the broken angularity which followed soon after in these accessories, when the influence of the school of Van Eyck began to be felt.

Lent by Mr. Fisher.

2.—The Turkish Emperor (coloured).

Probably printed at Augsburg, about 1470. Executed in a rude style.

Undescribed.

Lent by Mr. Mitchell.

3.—Two Leaves from a Biblia Pauperum,

The Bible Picture-Story-book of the poor, printed in the second half of the XVth century.

Lent by Mr. Mitchell.

3.*—The Bible, in Plat Deutsch of Cologne. Printed by Quentell, about 1475.

Lent by Mr. H. H. Gibbs.

ERHARD REUWICH.

4.—Frontispiece to Breydenbach's Travels in the Holy Land. Mayence, 1486.

(Pass. T. I. p. 63.) Bernhard von Breydenbach was a canon of Mayence. The title to his very remarkable work is treated in a masterly manner, superior to the rest of the illustrations of his book, and shews, for the first time in wood engraving, cross hatchings in the shadows, and very well executed. Erhard Reuwich, of Utrecht, designed, and also probably himself engraved, these cuts.

Lent by Mr. Mitchell.

PLEYDENWURFF and WOHLGEMUTH.

5.—NUREMBERG CHRONICLE, The Last Judgment, from this celebrated work, printed by A. Koberger at Nuremberg, in 1493.

The woodcuts are engraved from designs by Michael Wohlgemuth and Wilhelm Pleydenwurff, "painters and citizens of that town."

Lent by Mr. Fisher.

ANONYMOUS.

6.—MISSALE, Bamberg, 1499.

In case.

The volume lies open at a fine emblazoned and illuminated cut of the Crucifixion, on vellum.

Lent by Mr. H. H. Gibbs.

LUCAS CRANACH, b. 1470 (according to Bartsch: according to Passavant, 1472), in the Diocese of Bamberg, at Kronach, from which place he took his name.

In 1506 he entered the service of the Elector of Saxony, at Wittenberg; in 1519 he became a Member of Council, and Burgomaster in 1537. In 1550 he removed to Weimar, and thence to Augsburg in the following year, at the desire of the Elector, who was then a prisoner there. Cranach remained until the liberation of the Prince in 1552, and returned with him to Weimar, where he died, a year later, at the age of 81.

7.—ADAM AND EVE (B. 1).

Lent by Mr. Fisher.

8.—REPOSE IN EGYPT (B. 3).

Lent by Mr. Mitchell.

9.—REPOSE IN EGYPT (B. 4).

Lent by Mr. Fisher.

10.—CHRIST AND THE WOMAN OF SAMARIA (B. 22).

Lent by Mr. Fisher.

11.—ST. JOHN PREACHING (B. 60).

Lent by Mr. Mitchell.

12.—ST. JEROME (B. 63).

Lent by Mr. Mitchell.

13.—St. George (B. 65).

This is a remarkable example of early printing in colour and gold by the reputed father of that style. The print was discovered not long ago in Vienna; and it confirms the conjecture of Schuchardt and Herberger that this kind of printing was invented by Cranach.

Lent by Mr. Mitchell.

14.—St. Ursula, with other Saints.

Below are printed the rules and privileges of the Brotherhood of St. Ursula at Braunau, in Bavaria, with the statement that Dr. Ulrich Pinder had published a book on the subject at Augsburg.

Undescribed.

Lent by Mr. Fisher.

15.—Saints adoring the Crucifix (B. 76).

Lent by Mr. Mitchell.

16.—Venus and Cupid (B. 113).

First state, with the straight outline to the left shoulder of the goddess, which was afterwards rounded.

Printed in chiaro-oscuro from two blocks.

Lent by Mr. Mitchell.

17.—The Judgment of Paris (B. 114).

This print, according to Passavant, illustrates rather the passage of the legend, in which William of Albonach presents his three daughters to Alfred the Great, of England, that he may choose from them a wife.

Lent by Mr. Fisher.

18.—A Hunting Scene (B. 119).

Lent by Mr. Fisher.

19.—Two Tournaments, 1506 (B. 124), and 1506 (B. 125).

Lent by Mr Fisher.

20.—Luther, as "Master George," as he was called, when in hiding in the Wartburg (Schuchardt 179).

Lent by Mr. Mitchell.

21.—Melancthon.

Undescribed.

This cut is, probably, by the younger Cranach, the second son of the elder artist, born in 1515. His works have commonly been confused with those of his father.

Lent by Mr. Mitchell..

ALBRECHT DÜRER, b. May 20, 1471, at Nuremberg.

Till the age of 15 he remained as an apprentice with his father, a goldsmith. On his birthday, in 1486, he entered the *atelier* of M. Wohlgemuth. There he remained working four years, after which he began a tour through Germany, and met, at Colmar, the brothers of M. Schongauer; he then went to Venice, where he was in 1494. Returning in the same year, he married Agnes Frey. In 1506 and 1507 he re-visited Venice, and went on to Bologna. In 1520-21, he travelled in the Netherlands; and, worn out by the assiduity of his application and the vexatious, avaricious nature of his wife, he died of exhaustion, April 6, 1528, not yet 57 years of age.

It is improbable that Dürer ever himself executed any of his designs on the wood.

22.—PORTRAIT OF DÜRER (B. 156).

Second state.

Lent by Mr. Mitchell.

23.—SAMSON AND THE LION (B. 2).

Lent by Mr. Mitchell.

24.—ADORATION OF THE MAGI (B. 3).

Lent by Mr. Mitchell.

25.—THE TITLES TO THE LIFE OF THE VIRGIN AND THE GREAT PASSION (B. 4 and 76).

Printed upon a single sheet.

Lent by Mr. Mitchell.

26-31.—THE LARGE PASSION (B. 4-15).

    26.—The Last Supper (B. 5).
    27.—The Taking of Christ (B. 7).
    28.—The Bearing the Cross (B. 10).
    29.—Christ on the Cross (B. 11).
    30.—The Descent into Hades (B. 14).
    31.—The Resurrection (B. 15).

Six specimens of the series, which, complete, consists of 12 cuts.

Lent by Mr. Fisher.

32, 33.—THE SMALL PASSION (B. 16-52).

This set, which, complete, consists of 37 cuts, is here represented by six specimens. The first frame contains the "Adam and Eve eating the Forbidden Fruit" (B. 17); and "Adam and Eve driven from the Garden of Eden," in two states, the first extremely rare. The second frame contains four more cuts from the same series.

Lent by Mr. Fisher.

34.—THE SMALL PASSION (B. 16-52).

In case.

This is a copy of the second edition (1511), with Latin text.

Lent by Mr. Mitchell.

35.—THE LAST SUPPER (B. 53).

Lent by Mr. Mitchell.

36.—THE CRUCIFIXION, in a Border (B. 56).

Lent by Mr. Fisher.

37.—CHRIST ON THE CROSS, WITH ANGELS (B. 58).

This is printed from two blocks, joined together.

Lent by Mr. Fisher.

38, 39.—THE APOCALYPSE, the Titles of the German and Latin Editions (B. 60).

Lent by Mr. Fisher.

40.—THE APOCALYPSE, Title (B. 60).

A proof, before the letterpress.

Lent by Mr. Mitchell.

41.—THE MARTYRDOM OF ST. JOHN (B. 61).

A proof, from the Apocalypse.

Lent by Mr. Mitchell.

42.—THE FOUR RIDERS (B. 64).

A proof, from the Apocalypse.

Lent by Mr. Mitchell.

43.—THE SCARLET WOMAN (B. 73).

A proof, from the Apocalypse.

Lent by Mr. Mitchell.

44.—THE BEAST WITH RAM'S HORNS (B. 74).

A proof, from the Apocalypse.

Lent by Mr. Mitchell.

45.—THE ANGEL CLOSING THE ABYSS (B. 75).

A proof, from the Apocalypse.

Lent by Mr. Mitchell.

46-64.—THE LIFE OF THE VIRGIN (B. 76-95).

    (Title, The Virgin, seated on a crescent,—see No. 25.)

        46.—The High Priest excluding Joachim from the Altar (B. 77).
        47.—The Angel appearing to Joachim (B. 78).
        48.—Joachim embracing St. Anne (B. 79).
        49.—The Birth of the Virgin (B. 80).
        50.—The Presentation of the Virgin (B. 81).
        51.—The Espousal of the Virgin (B. 82).
        52.—The Annunciation (B. 83).
        53.—The Visitation (B. 84).
        54.—The Nativity (B. 85).
        55.—The Circumcision (B. 86).
        56.—The Adoration of the Kings (B. 87).
        57.—The Presentation in the Temple (B. 88).
        58.—The Flight into Egypt (B. 89).
        59.—The Repose in Egypt (B. 90).
        60.—Christ disputing with the Doctors (B. 91).
        61.—Christ taking leave of His Mother (B. 92).
        62.—The Death of the Virgin (B. 93).
        63.—The Assumption of the Virgin (B. 94).
        64.—The Virgin adored by Saints (B. 95).

    These are all of the First Edition.

Lent by Mr. Fisher.

65.—THE HOLY FAMILY (B. 96).

Lent by Mr. Mitchell.

66.—THE HOLY FAMILY (B. 97).

Lent by Mr. Mitchell.

67.—THE VIRGIN, WITH ANGELS (B. 101).

Lent by Mr. Mitchell.

68.—THE HOLY FAMILY, in a landscape, with rabbits in the foreground (B. 102).

Lent by Mr. Fisher.

69.—ST. CHRISTOPHER (B. 103).

Lent by Mr. Mitchell.

70.—THE TEN THOUSAND MARTYRS (B. 117).

Lent by Mr. Mitchell.

71.—THE MARTYRDOM OF ST. CATHERINE (B. 120).

Lent by Mr. Mitchell.

72.—THE TRINITY (B. 122).

Lent by Mr. Mitchell.

73.—THE DECOLLATION OF ST. JOHN (B. 125), and THE DAUGHTER OF HERODIAS (B. 126) RECEIVING THE HEAD OF ST. JOHN.

Lent by Mr. Mitchell.

74.—A MAN ON HORSEBACK (B. 131).

Lent by Mr. Mitchell.

75.—THE TRIUMPHAL CAR OF MAXIMILIAN (B. 138).

First sheet; second state.

Said to have been executed by Jerome Resch. The set, which consists of 92 blocks of different sizes, offers the very finest examples of woodcutting, and is of the greatest rarity.

Lent by Mr. Mitchell.

76.—THE EMPEROR MAXIMILIAN (B. 138).

This is a trial-proof of that portion of the first block of the series which contains the Emperor's portrait. Trial-proofs, such as this, are very rarely found, and are extremely interesting, as shewing the *modus operandi*.

Lent by Mr. Mitchell.

77, 78.—TWO DESIGNS FOR EMBROIDERY (B. 143 and 144).

The first of these is an impression taken before the cypher was engraved in the centre.

Lent by Mr. Mitchell.

79.—THE CELESTIAL GLOBE (B. 151).

Lent by Mr. Mitchell.

80.—The Portrait of the EMPEROR MAXIMILIAN (B. 153).

Lent by Mr. Fisher.

81.—The Portrait of ULRIC VARNBÜLER (B. 155).

Lent by Mr. Mitchell.

82.—THE THREE COATS OF ARMS OF NUREMBERG (B. 162).

Lent by Mr. Mitchell.

83.—THE ARMS OF L. STAIBER (B. 168).

Lent by Mr. Mitchell.

84.—THE HEAD OF CHRIST (B. App. 26).

    Attributed to Dürer.

Lent by Mr. Mitchell.

85.—THE VIERGE AUX CHARTREUX (Pass. 180).

Lent by Mr. Mitchell.

86.—A Title-page, with the arms of B. PIRKHEIMER (Pass. 205).

Lent by Mr. Mitchell.

87.—The same cut, on the title of BEATISS. PATRIS NILI, EPISCOPI ET MARTYRIS, Nuremberg, 1516.
In case.

Lent by Mr. Mitchell.

88.—Portrait of EOBANUS HESS (Pass. 218).

    Hess was born in 1488. He was a poet, and was appointed Professor of Poetry in the High School, which was established in Nuremberg in the year 1526. The original silver-point drawing for this woodcut, much injured, is in the British Museum.

Lent by Mr. Mitchell.

89.—THE EMPEROR MAXIMILIAN, WITH SAINTS, IN ADORATION (B. App. 32).

    In the rare first state, with the Latin inscriptions above and below, and before the block was split.

    Ascribed by Bartsch to Dürer.

Lent by Mr. Mitchell.

89.*—THE LEGEND OF ST. FRANCIS.

    Illustrated with woodcuts, executed (according to Hummel, "Neue Bibliothek," bd. 1, p. 1) by the printer, Hieronymus Höltzel, who published the book, in 8vo., at Nuremberg, in 1512.

    In case.

Lent by Mr. Mitchell.

HANS BURGMAIR, or BURGKMAIR, the elder, b. 1473, at Augsburg.

    At the age of 15 he was a pupil of M. Schongauer, at Colmar, but subsequently attached himself to the school, or at least to the following, of Dürer, with whom he was on terms of friendship. He is mentioned as already dead, in 1531, in the Register of Painters' Privileges (Gerechtigkeitsbuch), at Augsburg. His designs for woodcuts are very numerous.

90.—THE VIRGIN AND CHILD   11).

Lent by Mr. Mitchell.

91.—The Portrait of the EMPEROR MAXIMILIAN (B. 32).
Printed in chiaro-oscuro.

Lent by Mr. Mitchell.

92.—DEATH AND THE YOUNG MAN (B. 40).
In chiaro-oscuro.

Lent by Mr. Mitchell.

93.—THE THREE GOOD CHRISTIAN MEN AND WOMEN (B. 64, 65).
First state, before the architectural border.

Lent by Mr. Mitchell.

94.—THE THREE GOOD JEWS (B. 66).
Second state, with the border.

Lent by Mr. Mitchell.

95.—THE THREE GOOD HEATHEN MEN AND WOMEN (B. 68, 69).
First state, before the architectural border.

Lent by Mr. Mitchell.

96.—The Portrait of CONRAD CELTES (Pass. 118).

The person here represented was one of the leading German Humanists of the XVth century, and Professor at the University of Ingolstadt; he was called in 1497 to fill the chair of Poetry and Rhetoric at the University of Vienna, where he died in 1508. This portrait was executed in the year before his death, at his own request; and he gave impressions of it to his friends.

Lent by Mr. Mitchell.

97.—THE GREAT IMPERIAL EAGLE (Pass. 120).

This allegorical print refers to the *Collegium Poetarum et Mathematicorum*, instituted in 1501 by the Emperor Maximilian, in connection with the University of Vienna.

Lent by Mr. Mitchell.

98.—THE ARMS OF CARDINAL LANG (Ascribed to Burgmair).
Printed in colours.

Lent by Mr. Mitchell.

HANS BALDUNG, Surnamed GRÜN, b. about 1476, at Gmünd in Suabia.

He lived and painted at Lichtenthal in the Duchy of Baden, until 1533, when he removed to Strasburg, where he died in 1552. He was a friend of Dürer's, and his manner is partly formed on the style of that master.

99.—THE WITCHES (B. 55).

Dated 1510.

Lent by Mr. Fisher.

100.—THE VIRGIN AND CHILD (Pass. 66).

Lent by Mr. Mitchell.

101.—THE HOLY FAMILY, WITH ST. ANN (Pass. 67).

Lent by Mr. Mitchell.

102.—ST. JEROME (Pass. 70).

Printed in chiaro-oscuro.

Passavant does not mention any impression of this cut thus printed.

Lent by Mr. Mitchell.

103.—THE VIRGIN AND CHILD, WITH ST. ANN (attributed to H. Baldung).

This is copied from a drawing by A. Dürer, dated 1514, in the collection of Mr. Mitchell.

Lent by Mr. Mitchell.

NICOLAS MANUEL, surnamed DEUTSCH, b. in 1484, at Berne.

He became, in 1511, a Member of the Grand Council of Two Hundred; and, in 1528, he was a Member of the Select Council, and was employed frequently on missions, in quelling the disturbances caused by the Reformation movement. Drawings in pencil and oil, by his hand, exist; and he painted, in fresco, the Dance of Death for the Dominican Convent at Berne, 1515-21, his most important work. It appears that he did actually engrave on wood some, at least, of his compositions,—an uncommon practice among painters. He died at Berne, after a laborious and eventful life, in 1530.

104.—THE TWO FOOLISH VIRGINS (B. 6).

Lent by Mr. Mitchell.

URSE GRAF, b., probably, at Bâle, about 1485.

Passavant describes 13 engravings on copper by this artist, all unknown to Bartsch, and has added many to the list of his wooden cuts; he says also that he does not believe the catalogue to be complete, since Graf worked to a large extent for the publishers of Bâle and Strasburg.

105.—THE LORD'S PRAYER (Pass. 106-113).

In case.

First Edition, without text at the back of each print.

Lent by Mr. Mitchell.

106.—THE LORD'S PRAYER (Pass. 106-113).

Second Edition, with Latin text, by Erasmus. Basileæ, 1523.

In case.

Lent by Mr. Mitchell.

107.—A Figure representing the CANTON OF ST. GALL (Pass. 118-130).

This is one of a set which represents the Swiss Cantons. The set exists, complete, in the Bâle Museum.

Lent by Mr. Mitchell.

108.—AN AUTHOR PRESENTING HIS WORK TO THE POPE CLEMENT V. (Pass. 132.)

Lent by Mr. Mitchell.

109.—Title-page to the EPISTLES OF ERASMUS, with the border containing the figure of Humanitas (Pass. 144).

Lent by Mr. Mitchell.

HANS LEONHARD SCHÄUFELEIN, b. about 1485, at Nuremberg.

He studied under Dürer, and was already, in 1512, established at Augsburg, where he executed for the Emperor Maximilian the designs for the celebrated Teuerdanck. In 1515, he went to Nördlingen; and in the following year he married. He lived at Nuremberg for some time, after which he returned to Nördlingen, where he died in March, 1540. His widow married, subsequently, Hans Schwartz, of Oettingen, who still used Schäufelein's mark upon his own works.

110.—THE MUSICIANS (B. 103).

    This is the last of a set, called the Marriage-Dancers.

Lent by Mr. Mitchell.

111.—CHRIST BEARING THE CROSS.

    Undescribed.

Lent by Mr. Mitchell.

112.—A SAINT IN PRISON.

    Undescribed.

Lent by Mr. Mitchell.

113.—SPECULUM PASSIONIS D. N. JHESU CHRISTI, per doctorem Vdalricum Pinder, MCCCCCVII. Nuremberg.

    The cuts are by Schäufelein, whose mark appears on that at which the book lies open.

    In case.

Lent by Mr. H. H. Gibbs.

JOHANN WECHTLIN, or WÄCHTLE, of Strasburg, b. about 1485.

    This was a painter, whose works were, until lately, much better known than his name. He has been variously called "Le maître aux bourdons croisés," "Johann Ulrich Pilgrim," and "Pilgrimstab." His manner bears some likeness to that of Baldung, though wanting some of that artist's freedom and boldness of fancy.

114.—THE VIRGIN AND CHILD (B. 3).

Lent by Mr. Mitchell.

115.—ALCON OF CRETE, DELIVERING HIS SON FROM THE SERPENT (B. 9).

Lent by Mr. Mitchell.

ALBRECHT ALTDORFER, b. at Altdorf, near Landshut, in Bavaria, in 1488.

    He was probably a pupil of his father, also a painter, Ulrich Altdorfer, who, in 1491, renounced his rights of citizenship at Ratisbon. Albrecht returned thither again in 1511, and became in 1521 a Member of the Privy Council, and afterwards Superintendent of Buildings, in that town. In 1528 he refused the post of Burgomaster, to which he had been elected; he made his will on February 12, 1538, and died two days later. It appears likely that he himself executed some of his own designs on the wood.

116.—The Virgin and Child, with a Monk Kneeling (B. 49).

Lent by Mr. Mitchell.

117.—The Virgin and Child (B. 50).

Lent by Mr. Mitchell.

118.—The Great Font (B. 59).

Lent by Mr. Mitchell.

119.—The Judgment of Paris, 1511 (B. 60).

Lent by Mr. Mitchell.

MICHAEL OSTENDORFER, b. about 1490, at Gemau, near Ratisbon.

He was a pupil of A. Altdorfer, and lived and worked at Ratisbon from 1519 to 1559, in which latter year he died. He was probably the designer only, and not also the executant, of his woodcuts.

120.—The Pilgrimage to the old Church of the Beautiful Virgin of Ratisbon (Pass. 13).

This print represents an event which occurred in 1516. It is in an undescribed state, with a Latin inscription at foot.

There is in the Library at Coburg an impression of this curious and interesting cut, on which the following remarks appear, in the handwriting of Dürer:—" This spectre has arisen at Ratisbon against the Holy Scripture, and has been condemned by the Bishop, but is tolerated for the sake of temporal advantages. God help us, that we may become His own, not through dishonour, but through Christ Jesus. Amen."

Lent by Mr. Mitchell.

AMBROSIUS HOLBEIN, the elder brother of Hans Holbein.

He was born about 1492. In his style he approaches his famous brother, but is, as a painter, far from equalling him in clearness and force. Ambrose designed many borders for titles for the books published by the booksellers of Bâle.

121.—The Calumny of Apelles (Pass. 1).

On the Title to Maximi Tyrii . . . . Sermones.

Lent by Mr. Mitchell.

DANIEL HOPFER, b. about 1495.

He lived and worked as an engraver at Augsburg till 1549.

122.—A Title-page, Representing JACOB AND ESAU. 1512.
Undescribed.

Lent by Mr. Mitchell.

HANS SPRINGINKLEE, Painter and Designer.

An inmate of Dürer's house, where he learned his art. He made the drawings for his prints, but it is improbable that he ever actually executed a woodcut himself. He died in 1540.

123.—THREE RELIGIOUS SUBJECTS from the "Hortulus animæ cum horis beatæ Virginis, secundum consuetudinem Romanæ ecclesiæ, &c.," which was published by F. Peypus, at Nuremberg, in 1516, with 83 cuts, 50 of which are by Springinklee.

The three specimens here exhibited are undescribed proofs before the letterpress.

      7. Christ on the Mount of Olives.
      12. The Mater Dolorosa.
      13. The Death of the Virgin.

Lent by Mr. Mitchell.

124.—NATIVITY (B. 51).

This print appears in Koberger's Bible, and also in the New Testament published in 1524 by F. Peypus.

Lent by Mr. Mitchell.

125.—ST. JEROME (Pass. 64).

This also appeared in Koberger's Bible, 1519, as well as, afterwards, in the Prologue "Sci. Hieronymi in Pentateuchum" in the edition of 1521, and in the spurious "Luther's Bible" by Peypus, 1524.

Lent by Mr. Mitchell.

HANS HOLBEIN.

This great artist was the second son of a painter of the same name, and was born at Augsburg towards the end of the year 1497. In 1516, the father established himself with his three sons at Bâle, where he died about 1526. The young Holbein remained here, studying and painting, until 1526, when he paid his first visit to England. He returned to Bâle in 1529; but, having come back again to this country, he was recalled by the Council of Bâle, who offered him a fixed salary, which he accepted, in 1532. He enjoyed, however, for a long time the post of Court Painter to Henry VIII., and only twice revisited Switzerland before 1542, about which year he appears to have fixed his residence here; and here he remained until 1554, when he died, at London, of the plague. It is improbable that Holbein ever cut any of his designs upon the block, any more than did the other great designers of that time. Hans Lützelburger, surnamed Franck, was the best of the artists who executed this kind of work at Bâle; and he cut for Holbein the blocks of the Dance of Death, the full-length portrait of Erasmus, two dagger-sheaths, and other pieces.

126.—FIFTEEN SUBJECTS FROM THE OLD TESTAMENT, published by J. Frellon, at Lyons, in 1551 (Pass. 1).

The earliest editions, published 1538-1549, are of the greatest rarity. The complete set consists of 90; the cuts are executed by different hands.

Lent by Mr. Mitchell.

127, 128.—EIGHTEEN SUBJECTS OF THE DANCE OF DEATH.

The complete set consists of 58 cuts (Pass. T. iii., p. 362).

The present selected specimens are all proofs.

10.—Die Keyserin, *The Empress.*
11.—Die Küniginn, *The Queen.*
15.—Die Aptiszin, *The Abbess.*
16.—Der Edelmann, *The Nobleman.*
20.—Der Ratszherr, *The Councillor.*
24.—Die Nunne, *The Nun.*
25.—Das Altweib, *The Old Woman.*
27.—Der Rychmann, *The Capitalist.*
28.—Der Kaufmann, *The Merchant.*
29.—Der Schiffmann, *The Sailor.*
30.—Der Ritter, *The Knight.*
31.—Der Groff, *The Earl.*

32.—Der Altmann, *The Old Man.*
33.—Die Greffin, *The Countess.*
34.—Die Edelfrau, *The Lady.*
35.—Die Herzogin, *The Duchess.**
36.—Der Kramer, *The Shopkeeper.*
37.—Der Ackerman, *The Labourer.*

Lent by Mr. Mitchell.

129.—THE SAINTS PROTECTORS OF THE TOWN OF FRYBURG, IN BRISGAU (Pass. 26).

Upon the Title of the Book :—"Nüwe Stattrechten vnd Statuten der loblichen Statt Fryburg im Prisgaw gelegen. Gedruckt von Adam Petri 1519" (and 1520.) On the back are the arms of the town, with two lions for supporters.

Lent by Mr. Fisher.

130.—CHRIST THE TRUE LIGHT ; Headpiece of a Protestant Almanack published at Zurich in 1527 (Pass. 28).

This cut is evidently by the hand of Lützelburger.

Lent by Mr. Mitchell.

THE TRAFFIC IN INDULGENCES (Pass. 29).

A photograph from the impression in the Museum at Cambridge. Also by Lützelburger, but unsigned.

Lent by Mr. Mitchell.

131.—DAGGER-SHEATH, WITH THE FIGURE OF FORTUNE (Pass. 43).

Complete, with the hilt, which is very rare.

Lent by Mr. Mitchell.

132.—CRANMER'S CATECHISM, illustrated with four cuts by Holbein (Pass. 45-48).

Executed by an English artist.

In case.

Lent by Mr. Mitchell.

133.—THE UNFAITHFUL SHEPHERD, on the title of " A lytle treatise," London. 1548 (Pass. 49).

In case.

Lent by Mr. Mitchell.

---

* NOTE.—The monogram of Lützelburger appears on this print.

134.—The full length portrait of ERASMUS (Pass. 57).

First state.

A fair example of Lützelburger's cutting.

Lent by Mr. Fisher.

135.—The bust portrait of ERASMUS (Pass. 58).

A proof, before the letterpress at back.

Lent by Mr. Mitchell.

136.—The New Testament, containing the BAPTISM OF CHRIST on title (Pass. 69).

Basel, 1524.

In case.

Lent by Mr. Mitchell.

137.—Title-page to the New Testament, containing the figures of ST. PETER and ST. PAUL (Pass. 73).

Executed by Lützelburger.

Lent by Mr. Mitchell.

138.—THE TABLE OF CEBES, OR THE COURSE OF HUMAN LIFE (Pass. 90).

This cut was used as a title for several books; in the present instance it does duty for that of the "Cornucopiæ, seu Latinæ Linguæ Commentarii locupletissimi, N. Perotto, &c., Val. Curio. Bas. Anno 1532."

Lent by Mr. Mitchell.

139.—A FRIEZE, WITH PEASANTS CHASING A FOX (Pass. 99).

Upon the upper part of a title, consisting of four portions, the lowest of which represents

THREE COUPLES OF PEASANTS DANCING (Pass. 100).

The title is that of "BEATI CYRILLI...AD...THEODOSIUM EPISTOLA, JOANNE OECOLAMPADIO INTERPRETE," not mentioned by Passavant.

Lent by Mr. Mitchell.

140.—NINE LITTLE GENII AND CHILDREN (Pass. 103).

On the border of the title to the "Utopia" of Sir T. More. Bas. Froben. 1518. In the corners, at top, hang two tablets, upon which appear the syllables, HANS. HOLB., the name of the designer.

Lent by Mr. Mitchell.

141.—Title-page to the Annotations of Erasmus (Pass. 105).

With a border on the lowest member of which are seven children representing the liberal arts.

Lent by Mr. Mitchell.

142.—Seven Printers' Marks (Froschauer of Zurich) (Pass. 137, &c).

Lent by Mr. Mitchell.

143.—Four Printers' Marks (Bebelius of Bâle), and One Printer's Mark, Fortune standing on a Globe (Cratander).

The printers' marks of Bebelius include the rare undescribed first state, with the punning inscription, "Verdruck mich armen nit."

Lent by Mr. Mitchell.

144.—The Title-page to Coverdale's Bible.

In fac-simile by Harris.

Lent by Mr. Mitchell.

145.—The Title-page to Cranmer's Bible.

Ascribed to Holbein.

Lent by Mr. Mitchell.

146—Genethliacon illustrissimi Eäduerdi Principis Cambriæ, Lond. MDXLIII.

(Pass. 51-53).

In case.

The volume lies open at the last of the three little cuts which adorn it.

Lent by Mr. Mitchell.

HANS SEBALD BEHAM, b. in 1500, at Nuremberg.

A pupil of Dürer, he seems to have imitated the Italian style of his cousin, Bartel Beham. In consequence of the irregular life he led, he was compelled to quit his native place, and established himself at Frankfort, where he became an inn-keeper, and died in 1550.

147.—The Virgin and Child.

Undescribed.

Lent by Mr. Mitchell.

148.—THE VIRGIN AND CHILD, WITH ST. JOSEPH (B. 123).

First and second states. First state with the date, rare; it exists only in the British Museum and at Coburg, beside the impression here exhibited.

Lent by Mr. Mitchell.

149.—THE VILLAGE FEAST (B. 168).

The first sheet only, consisting of the two first portions; the second state, with the date 1535, but without Glockendon's address.

Lent by Mr. Mitchell.

150.—BIBLISCH HISTORIEN (Pass. 1-73).

In case.

Zu Franckfurt am Meyn, bei Christian Egenolph, MDXXXIII. This is the first edition, not cited by Passavant, but apparently known to Bartsch.

Lent by Mr. Mitchell.

151.—THE DANCE OF HERODIAS (Pass. 174).

Two woodcuts on one sheet.

Lent by Mr. Fisher.

152-6.—THE PLANETS.

The complete set consists of seven cuts.

    152.—Sol. (Pass. 181).

Lent by Mr. Fisher.

    153.—Saturn (Pass. 182).

Lent by Mr. Fisher.

    154.—Luna (Pass. 183).

Lent by Mr. Fisher.

    155.—Mercurius (Pass. 185).

Lent by Mr. Mitchell.

    156.—Jupiter (Pass. 186).

Lent by Mr. Mitchell.

157.—Title to the NEW TESTAMENT.

Undescribed.

Zu Franckfurt am Meyn, bei Christian Egenolph.

Lent by Mr. Mitchell.

MATHIAS GERON, OF LAUINGEN.

This master, who was both painter and designer, worked about the middle of the XVIth century, at Lauingen, in Bavaria, where he painted, in 1551, for the Hôtel de Ville, a picture representing the army of Charles V. before that town. He seems to have been a pupil of H. Burgmair, and not to have himself ever executed his designs upon the blocks.

158.—Two Subjects from the Apocalypse (Pass. 1). Both dated 1546.

These are part of a large series, of which 54 are in the Library of Wolfenbüttel dated from 1544 to 1558.

Lent by Mr. Mitchell.

ERASMUS LOY, b. about 1525.

He lived at Ratisbon, and was apparently a designer, and, perhaps, also a manufacturer of ornamental paper. The two sheets described below (160), with two others (also in Mr. Mitchell's possession), representing architectural designs, were sent to the Town Council of Ratisbon as specimens, with a petition that a privilege should be granted to the inventor, protecting his designs.

(See *Nagler's Künstler Lexicon.*)

159.—A Frieze.

Undescribed.

Lent by Mr. Mitchell.

160.—A Design for Wall-paper.

Lent by Mr. Mitchell.

JOST AMMAN, of Zurich, b. in 1539, d. at Nuremberg in 1591.

A very fertile designer, chiefly celebrated for his pen and pencil drawings, of which he is said to have executed a larger number than any other artist. These he published as woodcuts, some of which, perhaps, were actually executed by his own hand.

161.—The Tournament (B. 21).

This took place at Vienna, by order of the Emperor Maximilian II. The date 1565, with the artist's monogram, appears at top, near the right.

Lent by Mr. Mitchell.

Printed by Libri Plureos GmbH in Hamburg,
Germany